# The VIKINGS
## Invasion and Settlement

## by Ruth Owen

Consultant: Cassidy Croci
Centre for the Study of the Viking Age
University of Nottingham

Ruby Tuesday Books

# Map of the Viking World

ATLANTIC OCEAN

GREENLAND

Labrador Sea

NEWFOUNDLAND

ICELAND

Norwegian Sea

NORWAY

SWEDEN

DENMARK

SCOTLAND

North Sea

ENGLAND

IRELAND

Baltic Sea

RUSSIA

Caspian Sea

Black Sea

TURKEY

Constantinople

Mediterranean Sea

**Legend:**
- Viking homeland
- Viking settlements
- Viking raids
- Vikings in North America

N E S W

# Contents

# Terror from the Sea

**On 8th June 793, terror came to the tiny island of Lindisfarne on the northeast coast of England. Vikings!**

## A Peaceful and Holy Place

Lindisfarne was home to a monastery, and was a place of peaceful Christian worship and learning. A saint named St. Cuthbert was buried at Lindisfarne and his grave became a shrine.

Kings and nobles gave gifts of money and valuable objects to the monks. It was these treasures that the Vikings desired.

Ruins of the monastery at Lindisfarne

## Death and Destruction

The band of Viking warriors sailed from their icy homeland in the north of Europe. Then they unleashed a brutal attack on the defenceless people of Lindisfarne. They hacked the monks to death. They burned down buildings and stole the unguarded religious treasures.

Viking battle axes

## The North Men

At this time in history, most people were smaller than they are today. However, skeletons found in Viking burials show that some Viking men may have been 2 metres tall. They were fearsome fighters and did not fear death. To their victims, Viking warriors must have been the stuff of nightmares!

The Domesday stone, found at Lindisfarne, shows seven Viking warriors attacking with battle axes and swords.

## No One Is Safe

The raid on Lindisfarne was the Vikings' first major attack outside of their homeland in Scandinavia. One of England's holiest shrines had been desecrated. The people of Lindisfarne were horrified and confused. Why had God and St. Cuthbert not protected them?

As word of the Viking attack spread, shockwaves of fear swept through coastal communities throughout Europe.

## The Age of the Vikings had begun.

# The World of the Vikings

**The Age of the Vikings was a period in history that began more than 1000 years ago. It lasted from about AD 750 until about AD 1100.**

## The Viking Homeland

The Vikings, or **Norse** people, came from Scandinavia. Today, this part of northern Europe is made up of three countries — Norway, Sweden and Denmark.

## Survivors

The Vikings were raiders, warriors and skilful sailors. But they were also farmers. In the south of the Vikings' homeland there was flat, **fertile** land for growing crops and grazing animals. But in the north, life was much harder. Here, the Vikings had to farm rocky land that was surrounded by mountains.

When winter came to Scandinavia, temperatures plunged and the land was covered with snow and ice. Surviving in this freezing, harsh land made the Viking people determined and tough.

In parts of Sweden and Norway it is dark day and night for weeks at a time during winter. Just like Scandinavian people today, Viking families had to live through these cold, dark times.

The modern-day fishing village of Hamnøy in Norway

Like today's Scandinavians, people in Viking times built settlements on the coast in mountainous areas.

# People of the North

For hundreds of years, most of Europe was controlled by the Romans. The **Roman Empire** spread across Europe and lasted for about 500 years, from 27 BC to AD 476.

The Romans built cities and roads across their empire. The people they conquered lived under Roman law and many followed the Romans' religion of Christianity.

However, northern Europe was never conquered by Rome. The early Scandinavian tribes that lived here before the Vikings resisted invasion by Rome's huge armies.

The people of the north were left alone. They lived in their own way in small settlements led by chiefs. They followed their own rules and worshipped their own gods.

Cattle grazing on rocky land in Norway

# Life in a Viking Village

**The homes in Viking settlements were built from wood, stone or blocks of turf. They had roofs made of thatch or turf.**

Thatch is made from dried grasses.

Modern-day replicas of Viking homes

## A Viking Home

Inside a Viking home there was usually just one large room. It was dark, because there were no windows. Smoke filled the air from a fire in the centre of the room that heated the house and was used for cooking.

Bench seats and beds lined the walls. At night, people slept on a thick layer of dried heather under warm animal skins and rugs woven from wool.

**The Vikings enjoyed drinking mead. They made this strong, sweet drink from honey.** ▼

A reconstruction of life in a Viking home

Meat could be roasted on a spit or cooked over the fire in a stew pot.

Mead was drunk from a wooden cup or a cow's horn.

## Farmers and Craftspeople

The Vikings grew wheat, oats and barley, which were made into bread, porridge and beer. They also grew cabbages, beans, peas and onions. Viking families kept pigs, sheep, cattle, geese and chickens. In winter, a family's animals came inside and shared the house!

Some Viking men were expert carpenters who built boats. Others were smiths who turned iron into swords, axes and other weapons. They also made nails and rivets for boat-building, tools, belt buckles and cooking pots.

Cloud berries

Wild boar

## Hunting, Fishing and Foraging

Viking men caught fish and hunted with bows and arrows for many kinds of meat, including reindeer, wild boar, hares and ducks. Women and children foraged for wild foods, such as mushrooms, nuts, berries, wild garlic and seabird eggs.

Mushrooms

Wild garlic

## Caring for the Family

Viking women worked hard, too. They took care of young children, cooked meals for their families and baked bread. They milked the cows and made cheese. They also made their family's clothes.

Seabird eggs

# Viking Fashion and Fun

Historians can work out how the Vikings dressed by studying objects such as fragments of cloth, buckles, brooches and old documents.

## Viking Style

An Arab traveller and writer named Ahmad Ibn Fadlan wrote a detailed description of the Vikings he saw in AD 922 in the region that is now Russia. He described their clothes and jewellery. He also wrote that the men had tattoos and both men and women wore dark eye make-up.

Long linen under-dress

Flax

Long tunic

Yarn

Wool trousers

Leather shoes

Wool over-dress held in place with brooches

## Colourful Fabrics

Viking women made clothes from sheep's wool and linen. To make linen, the stems of flax plants were soaked in water until they became a soft mass of fibres that could be spun into yarn. Then the yarn was woven into cloth. The homemade wool and linen fabrics were dyed bright colours using dyes made from plants.

Both men and women wore rings, arm-rings and necklaces. Beads were made from glass, jet and chunks of **amber** found on the shores of the Baltic Sea. ▼

Viking necklaces

Amber

Jet

Viking brooch

▲ Vikings wore a fur, leather or wool cloak pinned on one shoulder with a brooch.

## Little Vikings

Viking children did not go to school. They helped out on the farm and learned about their history and gods by listening to stories and songs. Viking children played with wooden dolls, spinning tops and model boats.

## Viking Gamers

Vikings of all ages liked to play board games. In the game of Hnefatafl, the army of white pieces had to get their king to safety in one of the board's corners. The army of red or brown warriors tried to surround the king and stop him escaping.

▲ The Vikings made the playing pieces from bone, reindeer antlers and even walrus tusks.

Viking people played music and listened to long, exciting poems and sagas (stories). Passed down from storyteller to storyteller, the poems and sagas told of gods, heroes, giants, dwarves and the creation of the Viking world.

# In the Blood

By hunting, fishing and working hard on their farms, the Viking people were able to survive in their tough homeland. However, the Vikings were **ambitious** and they wanted more!

## Battle in the Blood

Before the Viking age people in Scandinavia lived in tribes across the north of Europe. For centuries these tribes fought each other for land and power. Going into battle held no fear for the Vikings — they had fighting and raiding in their blood.

▲ Early Scandinavians carved images of warriors and boats into rock.

## Ambition and Adventure

The Vikings knew that beyond their world there were better lands and incredible riches for any man brave enough to take them. Filled with determination and courage, raiding parties of Viking warriors would set sail to find wealth and adventure.

A fjord

## Sailing in the Blood

The Vikings also had sailing in their blood. Their homeland was surrounded by ocean and they often sailed around the rugged coast instead of travelling by land.

In some parts of Scandinavia deep, narrow waterways called **fjords** snake their way inland from the sea. The Vikings used the fjords to sail from place to place. Travelling by boat was easier than walking over rocky land and mountains.

### Ancient Sailors and Raiders

We know that fighting and sailing were important to early Scandinavians because they left behind rock carvings of warriors and huge stone circles made in the shape of ships. Some stone ships mark the graves of people who lived around 3000 years ago. Some of the dead were **cremated** and then any remaining pieces of bone were washed and buried beneath the stone **monuments**.

A Viking stone ship monument in Sweden

# Sailors and Longships

**The Vikings were skilful boat-builders and sailors. When they went exploring and raiding, they sailed in narrow, streamlined longships that could carry over 60 men. The largest ships could carry more than 100!**

## Designed For Attack

Viking ships could withstand crossing rough, open seas. But they could also sail in shallow water and be stealthily sailed along narrow rivers. This allowed bands of Viking raiders to make attacks on inland communities where people thought they would be safe.

## Wind and Muscle Power

A Viking longship was powered by the wind. When the wind dropped, the crew rowed hard to power their ship. **Archaeologists** have found marks on the skeletons of Viking men where their muscles attached to the bones. By studying these stress markers, scientists can see that the men developed powerful muscles from rowing.

### Life at Sea

During ocean voyages, the crew survived on water, bread brought from home and long-lasting, sundried fish. They also attacked coastal settlements to steal food and drink. At night, the men wrapped themselves in waterproof sleeping bags made from seal skins. Then they slept on the ship's deck, using the sail as a tent to cover the ship.

Sundried fish

The ship's large sail was square or rectangular. We know this because stone carvings have been found that show the design of Viking longships. No sails remain from this time, but it's likely they were woven from wool.

The ship was made of wood from oak trees.

A Viking ship often had the head of a dragon or another fierce creature carved on its prow. The Vikings believed it terrified the spirits of the lands they raided.

Viking sailors **navigated** by following directions passed on by earlier explorers. They sailed close to the coast and kept watch for landmarks. They also used the position of the Sun and stars to show them the way.

Warriors' shields

# A Way of Life and Death

**Viking warriors were not afraid of fighting to the death. They believed a heroic death allowed them to gain entry to Valhalla.**

## The Hall of the Fallen

Valhalla was a great golden hall with a roof made of spears and shields. Here a warrior spent his days fighting with other heroes. At night, his battle wounds were magically healed and he would feast on wild boar and mead alongside Odin, the leader of the Viking gods.

## A Heroic Death

To a Viking warrior, nothing was more terrible than being remembered as a coward. When a Viking died on the battlefield with honour and courage, his **reputation** for bravery never died and he would become a hero for all time.

## The God of Warriors

The Vikings worshipped many gods. Thor was the strongest of them all and the favourite god of warriors. Thor carried a hammer named Mjölnir that could flatten mountains and crush the skulls of giants.

The Viking god Thor

Mjölnir

When Thor put on his Girdle of Might, his strength grew.

## Into Valhalla

The Tjängvide image stone was discovered in Sweden. It shows dead warriors doing battle in Valhalla. A warrior, or possibly the god Odin, is handed a horn of mead by a supernatural maiden called a Valkyrie. The Valkyries chose who died on the battlefield and who entered Valhalla. Their name means "choosers of the fallen".

The name Valhalla means "hall of the fallen".

A dead warrior, or the god Odin, on horseback

Valkyrie

This iron helmet from the late 900s was found in a Viking grave.

A replica Viking shield

## Into Battle

Warriors fought with daggers, axes, swords and spears. They carried a round wooden shield that was about 85 cm wide. Most warriors went into battle in their normal clothes, but some wealthy men may have worn a chainmail tunic and a metal helmet.

Viking sword

Metal chainmail

# Under Attack!

In the early morning darkness, a Viking longship would glide up onto a beach. Asleep in their beds, the Vikings' victims had no warning that death and destruction were heading their way.

Fore-stem of ship

# A Quick Getaway

A Viking longship had a fore-stem and an after-stem. This meant it could go forwards or backwards without turning around. A raiding party would leave their ship in shallow waters on a beach. Once the raid was over, the ship could simply be pushed back out to sea for a quick getaway.

## Slavery or Death

Sometimes the Vikings raided coastal villages to steal money, food, clothes, tools and weapons. They might even take prisoners and hold them to **ransom**. If people fought back, the Vikings did battle with their swords, axes and spears. Often the victims had no way to protect themselves. Then the defenceless men, women and children were captured to become slaves or they were murdered.

## Incredible Riches

At other times, Viking raiders descended on a monastery or church. These buildings were home to gold, silver, jewels, books, wines and beautiful textiles. The raiders knew that the nuns, monks and priests in these holy places would have no weapons to defend themselves.

Items like this gold and silver chalice could be melted down to make jewellery.

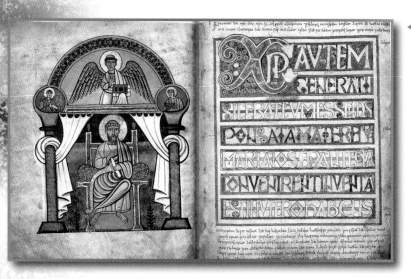

The Vikings realised that some items, such as bibles and other special books, could be held to ransom as a way to make money. The Codex Aureus is a book of Christian writings that was stolen during a Viking raid in Kent, England. Notes inside the book record that an **Anglo-Saxon** nobleman paid pure gold in exchange for the book's safe return.

The Codex Aureus is decorated with gold and silver.

# Traders and Slavers

**Viking warriors attacked settlements around the coast of mainland Europe. They also carried out raids on England, Scotland and Ireland.**

## Viking Kidnappers

The raiders didn't just steal treasure and goods — they also captured people! Their captives became thralls, or slaves, who could be used to do work or treated as goods to be sold.

## A Slave Market

In AD 841, the Vikings built a settlement and trading centre in Ireland. It became one of the largest slave markets in Europe. Today, that settlement is Ireland's capital city, Dublin.

A Viking trader selling a female slave to Arab **merchants**

## Doing Business

The Vikings didn't travel to distant places only to raid. They were also good business people who travelled far and wide, buying and selling goods.

Some Vikings headed east, their ships filled with animal furs, amber and slaves. Travelling by river, they sailed through Russia doing business along the way. Some traders took their families with them and settled in this new land.

Viking slave traders may have made their captives wear iron collars.

## Silk and Spices

Viking traders also visited the busy markets of Constantinople (modern-day Istanbul in Turkey). Here they sold their cargo and bought silks, spices, glassware and other goods from the Middle East and Asia. Then the traders sailed back to Scandinavia, loaded with exotic items that could be sold to wealthy Vikings.

Colourful spices for sale in an Istanbul market – just like in Viking times

Thousands of silver coins, called dirhams, have been discovered in Viking graves. They were from the region that is now modern-day Iraq and Iran. This shows that Viking traders did business with Arab merchants.

# Viking Invaders

**While some Vikings settled in the places they raided, usually they attacked and then headed home. In the late 800s, this all changed. The Vikings became invaders and rulers!**

## A Viking Army

The Vikings knew that Anglo-Saxon England was a wealthy country. They also knew that its lush, green land was a good place to live and farm. In AD 865, a huge army of Viking warriors (possibly up to 3000 men) landed on the shores of East Anglia. Led by powerful **warlords**, the Vikings had not come for treasure or slaves. This time, they had come for everything!

## To War

During this period England was divided into four kingdoms that were each ruled by an Anglo-Saxon king. For more than 10 years, the Vikings fought the Anglo-Saxons. They took control of the kingdoms of East Anglia, Northumbria and Mercia. Finally, only the kingdom of Wessex, ruled by King Alfred the Great, remained unconquered.

## The Anglo-Saxons

In the early 400s, people from Germany, the Netherlands and Denmark settled in England. According to the Anglo-Saxon Chronicle (a collection of historical records), they belonged to groups called the Angles, Saxons and Jutes. Together they are known as the Anglo-Saxons.

### Map of the Danelaw

North Sea

Anglo-Saxon Northumbria

Jorvik (York)

Irish Sea

Mercia

Wessex

Danelaw
Anglo-Saxon England
Areas controlled by different Celtic groups

## The Danelaw

Following many battles, King Alfred and the Viking leader Guthrum agreed to a **peace treaty**. The Vikings would leave Wessex, but take control of a large area of England. The Viking part of England was called the **Danelaw**.

## The Battle for England

In time, some of the Viking invaders married Anglo-Saxons and the languages and cultures of the two peoples became mixed. But the Anglo-Saxons and Vikings did not always live in peace. Throughout the next 200 years, they would go into battle many times in an ongoing struggle to control England.

The Anglo-Saxons called the Viking invaders "The Great Heathen Army". The word "heathen" meant someone who was not a Christian. ▼

## Speaking Viking

The blending of the Anglo-Saxon and Viking languages gave us many English words we use today.

| | | | |
|---|---|---|---|
| anger | give | reindeer | take |
| egg | happy | shake | trust |
| get | ill | sky | ugly |

## The Danegeld

Sometimes Anglo-Saxon kings tried to avoid war by paying the Viking invaders large amounts of silver to leave them in peace. These payments were called Danegeld, which means "Dane tribute, or payment". The kings often collected the Danegeld as tax from their people. Sometimes, however, the Vikings took the payment and attacked anyway!

# Jorvik: A Viking City

**One of the main Viking cities was Jorvik. Today, this city is called York.**

### Uncovering Jorvik

In the 1970s, a new shopping centre was being built in York on a street called Coppergate. This gave archaeologists a chance to see what lay beneath the city. They dug down through 9 metres of soil and **excavated** thousands of items from the Viking age. Their finds included human skeletons, remains of buildings and even shoes.

A Viking leather shoe

### A Viking Shopping Centre

The archaeologists discovered that many of the Viking residents of Coppergate were craftspeople. The goods they made included pottery, glassware, metal tools and jewellery. They lived in small wooden houses with a stall on the street where they sold their goods. Behind their homes were workshops and backyards where they kept pigs, geese and chickens.

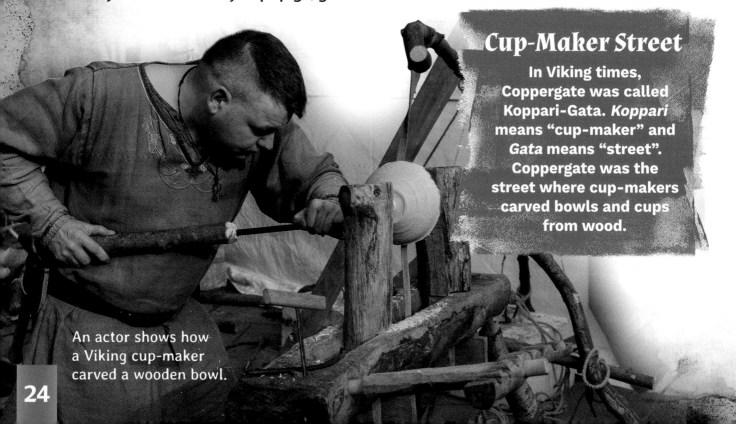

## Cup-Maker Street

In Viking times, Coppergate was called Koppari-Gata. *Koppari* means "cup-maker" and *Gata* means "street". Coppergate was the street where cup-makers carved bowls and cups from wood.

An actor shows how a Viking cup-maker carved a wooden bowl.

**Even Rubbish Tells a Story**

Behind each Viking home was a rubbish pit. By examining the 1000-year-old rubbish the archaeologists could learn what people in Jorvik ate. They found bones from sheep, cows and fish, oyster shells, walnuts, remains of wheat and barley and even cherry stones.

◀ Bones found at Coppergate show the Vikings kept dogs and cats. Unfortunately, they also shared their homes with lots of rats and mice!

Cat skull

## A Smelly City

Life in Jorvik was unhealthy and very smelly. There was no running water and people went to the toilet in holes in the ground behind their homes. Archaeologists found human **faeces** that contained large amounts of eggs from **parasitic worms**. Viking people would have become very ill if they had worms in their digestive systems.

The Vikings used handfuls of moss as toilet paper.

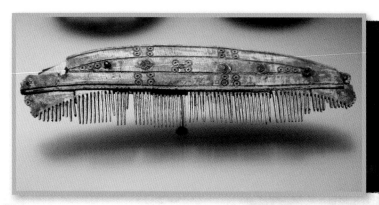

## Itchy and Scratchy

Lots of Coppergate craftspeople made combs that were used for grooming and for getting rid of itchy head lice!

Viking combs were carved from animal bones and antlers.

# Viking Explorers

As the Viking population grew, land became scarce in the rocky, mountainous north of their homeland. Some Vikings took to the seas searching for new places to settle.

## Icelandic Vikings

Some Viking explorers settled on the Shetland and Orkney Islands to the north of Scotland. And then in the late 800s, Viking adventurers braved the wild, dangerous Atlantic Ocean, sailing north to settle on Iceland.

The settlers survived by catching fish, walrus, seals and whales. They also brought farm animals with them from home. The animals grazed on grass and on seaweed that the Vikings gathered from the coast.

The rugged coast of Iceland

## The First Icelanders

In 2018 scientists studied the remains of 27 early Icelandic settlers. They took **DNA** samples from the teeth of the skeletons. By analysing the DNA they discovered that the settlers were Scandinavian, Irish and Scottish. They believe this evidence shows that the Viking settlers brought slaves with them to Iceland from Ireland and Scotland. The majority of the Irish and Scottish skeletons were female.

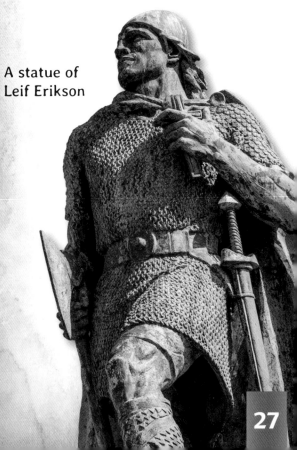

Shark meat air-drying in Iceland

## Rotten Shark

One food enjoyed by Icelandic Vikings was raw, rotten shark called hákarl. Shark meat contains toxins that could kill a person. Therefore chunks of shark were buried in sand and allowed to rot so the poisons oozed out. Then the meat was air dried. Some people in Iceland still eat this traditional Viking food today.

A replica of a Viking house in Iceland made from blocks of turf

# Adventure in the Blood

The Vikings continued to explore and search for new places to settle.

A Viking named Erik Thorvaldsson (Erik the Red) sailed from Iceland to Greenland. He explored the island and decided it would be a good place to settle.

Around the year AD 985, Erik led a fleet of 25 ships from Iceland to Greenland. Only 14 of the ships carrying Viking settlers survived the dangerous voyage.

Erik's son Leif Erikson was also an explorer. Some time around AD 1000, he sailed to Newfoundland, in modern-day Canada. The Vikings called this land Vinland. At this time, no other Europeans knew that North America existed.

Leif and his crew may even have explored other parts of North America's east coast.

A statue of Leif Erikson

# Into the Afterlife

**When life came to an end, a Viking was buried with the things he or she would need in the next life.**

## A Viking Ship Burial

Some Viking warriors, chiefs and other important people were buried on a ship inside a giant mound of earth.

In 1903, a farmer in Norway discovered a Viking ship when he dug into a burial mound on his land. Named the Oseberg Ship, it contained the bodies of two women. They were laid on a bed inside a small chamber on the deck of the ship.

## Ready for the Afterlife

The women were buried with sleighs, furniture, cooking equipment, tools, clothes, shoes, beads and food. The bodies of six dogs, two cows and 15 horses were also found on the ship. In Viking times animals were often **sacrificed** and buried with their owners so they could accompany them into the afterlife.

The Oseberg Ship is 21.5 metres long. It was designed to be rowed by 30 men.

## A Viking Mystery

Who were the women on the Oseberg Ship? No one knows. But their grand burial tells us that one or both of the women were important members of Viking society.

### The Oseberg Ship Women

The older of the two women on the Oseberg Ship was Scandinavian and about 80 years old when she died. By studying her bones, scientists can see that she was probably suffering from cancer. The second woman was about 50 years old and may have come from the Middle East.

# The Repton Warrior

The skeleton of a Viking invader was found buried in the English town of Repton. He was part of the great Viking army that invaded England. The warrior died from spear wounds to his head. He was buried with his sword and two knives so he could do everlasting battle in the Viking heaven of Valhalla.

Scientists used the warrior's skull to create this model of his face.

# Runestones

The Vikings invented an alphabet of letters called runes. The letters were designed with straight lines that could be carved into stone or wood. The names and deeds of some Viking warriors and explorers were carved onto runestones so they could be remembered for all time.

The oak ship is covered with intricate carvings of animals and sea serpents.

# Glossary

**amber**
Fossilized resin from prehistoric trees. Honey-coloured chunks of amber are cut and polished to make gemstones and beads for jewellery-making.

**ambitious**
Having a strong wish to be successful, powerful or rich.

**Anglo-Saxon**
Belonging to or having to do with a group of people who lived in Britain from the 400s onward. They originally migrated to Britain from Germany, Denmark and the Netherlands.

**archaeologist**
A scientist who studies the past by examining the physical remains left behind, for example buildings, skeletons and artefacts such as coins and weapons.

**cremate**
To dispose of a dead body by burning it until it has become ashes.

**Danelaw**
The part of England that was under the control of the Vikings. The area was roughly to the north of a line that ran from London up to Chester in Cheshire.

**DNA**
The material that carries all the information about how a living thing will look and function. DNA is short for deoxyribonucleic acid.

**excavate**
To dig out or remove something from soil or rock.

**faeces**
Another word for waste or poo.

**fertile**
When describing land or soil: able to produce lots of crops.

**fjord**
A long, deep waterway that leads from the sea into the land. A fjord has high cliffs on each side.

**merchant**
A person (usually from history) who buys and sells goods. Merchants often travelled from place to place to do business.

**monument**
A statue, building or other structure that is erected to commemorate a person or event.

**navigate**
To plan and then guide the direction that a ship, or other vehicle, takes from one place to another.

**Norse**
Having to do with the people of Scandinavia in ancient or Medieval times. For example, the Vikings are also known as Norse people and they worshipped Norse gods.

**parasitic worm**
A type of worm that lives in and feeds on a person or animal.

**peace treaty**
An agreement, made between two countries or groups of people, to stop fighting a war.

**ransom**
To take someone prisoner and demand money in return for their release.

**reputation**
A belief about someone that is believed by many people and is based on a particular kind of behaviour. For example, a warrior's reputation as a hero would be based on his brave actions in battle.

**Roman Empire**
The parts of the world that were conquered and ruled over by the Romans. The empire included Italy and parts of Europe, North Africa and the Middle East.

**sacrifice**
To kill an animal or person as part of a ritual or as an offering to a god.

**warlord**
A military leader.

# Index

## A
amber 11, 21
Anglo-Saxons 19, 22—23
archaeologists 14, 24—25

## B
burials and graves 4, 5, 13, 17, 21, 28—29

## C
children 9, 11
clothes 9, 10—11, 17, 28
Codex Aureus book 19
Constantinople 21
Coppergate, York 24—25
craftspeople 9, 24

## D
Danegeld 23
Danelaw 22
death 5, 16—17, 28—29
DNA 26
Dublin 20

## E
early Scandinavians 7, 12
England 4—5, 19, 20, 22—23, 29
Erikson, Leif 27
explorers 14—15, 26—27, 29

## F
Fadlan, Ahmad Ibn 10
farming 6—7, 9, 12, 22, 26
fishing 9, 12, 26
fjords 13
food and drink 8—9, 14, 16—17, 19, 25, 26—27, 28

## G
games 11
gods 11, 16
Great Heathen Army 23, 29
Greenland 27
Guthrum 22

## H
hákarl 27
houses 8—9, 24—25, 27
hunting 9, 12, 26

## I
Iceland 26—27
invading 22—23, 29
Ireland 20, 26

## J
jewellery 10—11, 19, 24
Jorvik 24—25

## K
King Alfred the Great 22

## L
language 23
Lindisfarne, England 4—5

## M
money 19, 21
monuments 13

## N
Newfoundland 27

## O
Odin 16—17
Oseberg Ship 28—29

## R
raiding 4—5, 6, 12—13, 14—15, 18—19, 20—21, 22
ransoming 19
Repton warrior 29
runes 29
runestones 29
Russia 10, 21

## S
sacrifices 28
sailing 6, 12—13, 14—15, 27
Scandinavia 5, 6—7, 12—13, 21, 26, 28
Scotland 20, 26
ships 9, 12—13, 14—15, 18—19, 21, 27, 28—29
skeletons 5, 14, 24, 26, 28—29
slaves 19, 20—21, 22, 26

## T
Thor 16
Thorvaldsson, Erik 27
toilets 25
traders 20—21
treasure 4, 12, 19, 20, 22

## V
Valhalla 16—17, 29
Valkyries 17
villages 8—9

## W
warriors 4—5, 6, 12, 16—17, 18—19, 20, 22—23, 28—29
weapons 4—5, 9, 17, 29
women 8—9, 10—11, 28

## Y
York 24